PRESENTED TO:

_____

FROM:

_____

DATE:

_____

From God's Heart to Yours

ROY LESSIN

eagle

Bath, England

Unless otherwise indicated, all Scripture quotations are taken from the King James Version of the Bible.

Scripture quotations marked NIV are taken from the *New International Version*, copyright © 1973, 1978, 1984 by International Bible Society. Used by permission of Hodder & Stoughton, a Division of Hodder Headline.

Scripture quotations marked TLB are taken from *The Living Bible*, copyright © 1971, 1988 by Tyndale House Publishers Inc, Wheaton, Illinois 60189, USA.

From God's Heart to Yours
ISBN 0 86347 566 3
Copyright © 2001 by Roy Lessin
First published by RiverOak Publishing, P O Box 700143, Tulsa, Oklahoma 74170, USA

This edition published 2003 by
Eagle Publishing Ltd, 6 Kestrel House, Mill Street, Trowbridge, Wilts BA14 8BE.

British Library Cataloguing in Publication Data. A catalogue record for this book is available from the British Library.

All rights reserved. No part of this publication may be reproduced or transmitted in any form or by any means, electronic or mechanical, including photocopying, recording or any information storage and retrieval system, without either prior permission in writing from the publisher or a licence permitting restricted copying. In the United Kingdom such licences are issued by the Publishers Licensing Society Ltd, 90 Tottenham Court Road, London W1P 9HE

Designed by Greg Jackson, Jackson Design Company, Siloam Springs, Arkansas
Greg@jacksondesignco.com

Illustrated by Todd Williams

Typeset by Eagle Publishing Ltd
Printed by Book Print SL, Spain

From God's Heart to our hearts, He gives generously—joy, glory, grace, kindness, power, faith, promises, love. We start this life receiving everything from the tender heart of God—our bodies formed by His hand, our spirits quickened by His breath. We daily receive of His bounty: The air we breathe, the water we drink, the seeds we plant are all given to us by our Creator God.

When we become God's children in Christ, once again we become receivers. Our life is of Him, through Him, and to Him. The greatest gifts are ours—forgiveness, eternal life, the Holy Spirit, and fellowship with God—when we become joint heirs with Christ and members of His body, the Church. We receive grace and mercy, comfort and hope, the fruit and gifts of His Spirit, and the boldness we need to overcome all that is contrary to His goodness.

It is only as we receive these rich blessings from God's heart that we can give the gift of His love to others. Abundant blessings are given to us so that we can become generous givers—from God's heart to ours to others. The rivers of living water are to flow out from our innermost being. The seeds in our hands are to be scattered abroad. The love that has come from His heart is to be shared with all.

— ROY LESSIN —

Freely ye have received, freely give.
MATTHEW 10:8

ROY LESSIN

The Lord bless you and keep you.

NUMBERS 6:24 NIV

FROM GOD'S HEART TO YOURS

What could be better than God blessing you!

~

It is goodness coming to you
from the Father of all that is good,
sunshine from the Father of all lights,
hugs from the Father of all mercies.

~

When He keeps you,
He places you close to His heart to warm you.
He sets His eye upon you
and watches over you without ever sleeping.
He covers you with His wings
to shield you from the storms of life.

~

His blessing
is the lift to your step,
the smile to your face,
the song to your heart.

~

How blessed you are to be blessed of Him!

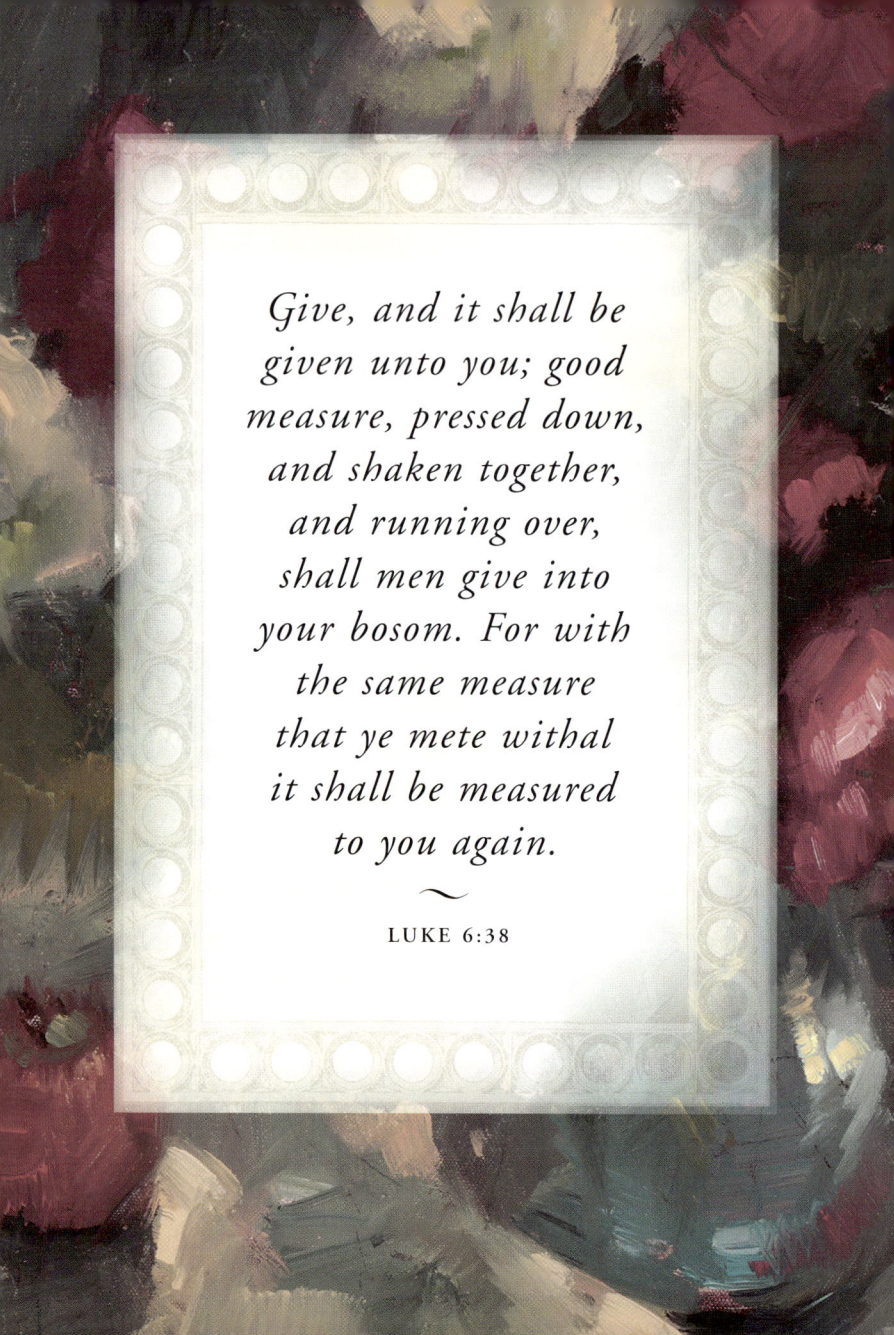

Give, and it shall be given unto you; good measure, pressed down, and shaken together, and running over, shall men give into your bosom. For with the same measure that ye mete withal it shall be measured to you again.

LUKE 6:38

FROM GOD'S HEART TO YOURS

As long as you are giving away the things that God has given you, you can never be empty. His provisions are limitless; His grace is endless; His love is boundless. He will always replace what you have given and return to you in even greater measure the things you have given away.

*The Lord make his face shine
upon you and be gracious to you.*

NUMBERS 6:25 NIV

*T*he Lord's face is the most lovely to gaze upon.

∼

It is the face of unending brightness.
As it shines upon you,
it burns away the fog of confusion.
It moves away the clouds of doubt
that cause you to question His love.
It dispels the darkness
that causes your heart to fear.

∼

His is not a brooding face,
but a face as calm as a sea of glass.
His is not a hollow face,
but a face strong in character,
compassion, and grace.

∼

Grace for you to grow in,
grace for you to rest in,
grace for you to joy in.
Grace upon you,
grace within you,
grace around you
—flooding you with holy light!

ROY LESSIN

*I will make of thee
a great nation,
and I will bless thee,
and make thy name great;
and thou shalt be a blessing.*

GENESIS 12:2

God has blessed you to make you a blessing.

~

He wants to give through your hands,
smile through your face,
care through your heart,
speak through your voice,
and shine through your eyes.

~

Like bread,
He will break you and multiply you.

~

Like a cup of cool water,
He will pour you forth.

~

Like a well-planted tree,
He will make you fruitful to every good work.

*The Lord turn his face
toward you
and give you peace.*

~

NUMBERS 6:26 NIV

*N*othing is better than living under God's approval—to see His smile upon your life, to make His heart glad, to cause Him to joy over you with singing, to have Him say of you, "This is My child in whom I am well pleased."

~

He wants you to please Him as a child pleases a father. You please Him with the spontaneity of your love, with the abandonment of your trust, with the completeness of your obedience. His peace rests with His approval.

~

As you go through this day, make no decision, entertain no thought that will move you away from that peace.

ROY LESSIN

*He must increase,
but I must decrease.*

~

JOHN 3:30

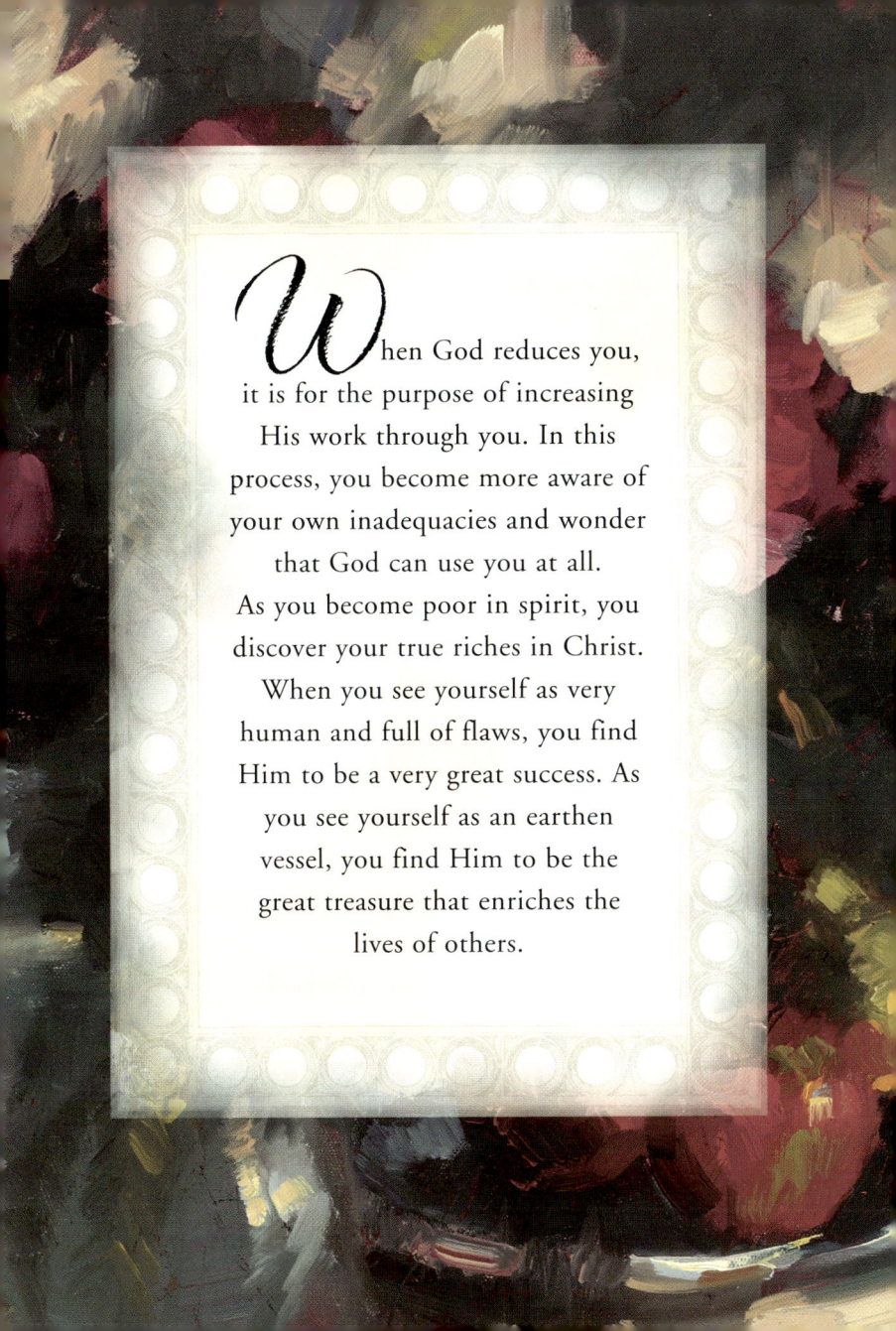

When God reduces you, it is for the purpose of increasing His work through you. In this process, you become more aware of your own inadequacies and wonder that God can use you at all. As you become poor in spirit, you discover your true riches in Christ. When you see yourself as very human and full of flaws, you find Him to be a very great success. As you see yourself as an earthen vessel, you find Him to be the great treasure that enriches the lives of others.

ROY LESSIN

*The blessing of the Lord,
it maketh rich, and he
addeth no sorrow with it.*

~

PROVERBS 10:22

The blessings of God come to you freely as His child.

~

God's blessings enrich you without your working to receive them. They bring no guilt or condemnation, no regrets or heaviness, no bondage or shame. God wants you to enjoy His blessings, to receive them with a thankful heart, and to use them for the highest good. They are gifts of His grace. He does not "balance them out" with bad things to keep you from enjoying them too much!

ROY LESSIN

From the time he put him in charge of his household and of all that he owned, the Lord blessed the household of the Egyptian because of Joseph. The blessing of the Lord was on everything Potiphar had, both in the house and in the field.

GENESIS 39:5 NIV

God will bless the lives of others
because His blessing is upon you.

You don't have to make a difference,
because you will be a difference
as you walk humbly and obediently with God.

Others will glorify the Father because of you.

When God moves you
into a new relationship or job,
the lives of others
will be affected for good
in a way that never
would have happened
had you not been there.

ROY LESSIN

*The Lord your God will bless you
as he has promised, and
you will lend to many nations
but will borrow from none.
You will rule over many nations
but none will rule over you.*

DEUTERONOMY 15:6 NIV

An authority and a freedom are included in the blessings of God in your life. Dependency upon God frees you from dependency upon others. You can stand tall, look others in the eye, and never be ashamed when your trust is in the Lord. He makes you the head and not the tail. He makes you a leader who sees the way, not as the blind leading the blind. He causes you to speak with authority, not as one whose words fall to the ground.

ROY LESSIN

Saul's son Jonathan went to David at Horesh and helped him find strength in God.

1 SAMUEL 23:16 NIV

*I*t is a blessing to others when
God sends you to them
as a voice of encouragement.

When they fear the future,
you can bring a word of hope.
When they question the past,
you can bring an assuring answer.
When they wonder
how they can face the day,
you can speak a word of faith.

God will use you to help others to press on,
to persevere, to remain faithful.
He will send you as a friend with words spoken from the
heart, as an ambassador with a message from the King,
and as a fellow pilgrim in whose eyes
shine the light of the celestial city.

*Behold, I have received
commandment to bless:
and he hath blessed;
and I cannot reverse it.*

NUMBERS 23:20

The blessings of God upon you are greater than any curse the enemy would try to put upon you. The blessings of Jesus' victory over Satan are your victory.

~

Jesus destroyed the works of the devil so He might do His good work in you. Jesus exposed the enemy's lies so His truth would triumph through you. Jesus broke the power of the evil one's authority so He would reign as the Lord of your life.

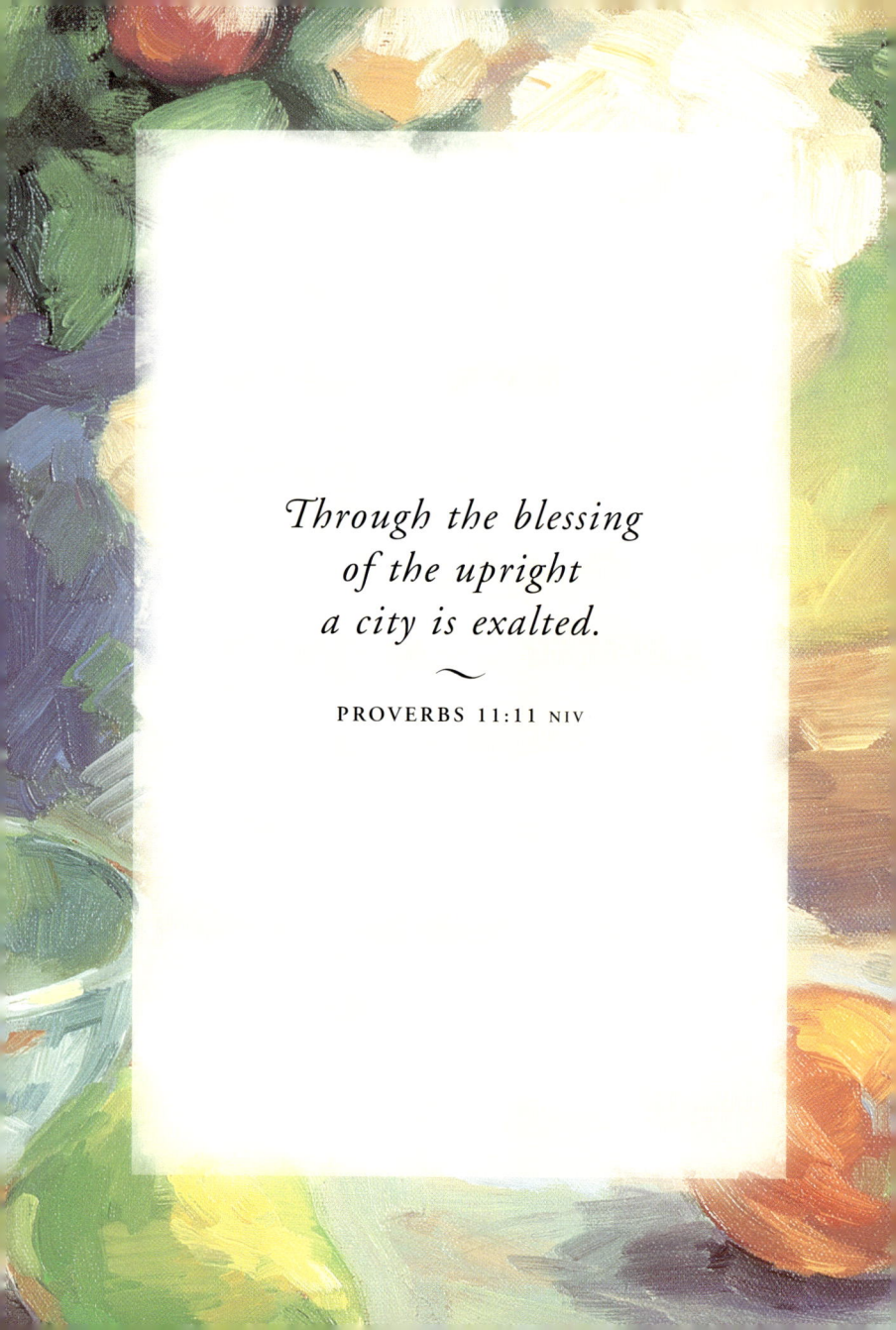

*Through the blessing
of the upright
a city is exalted.*

PROVERBS 11:11 NIV

FROM GOD'S HEART TO YOURS

*T*he place where you live is blessed because you are there.

> Having your citizenship in Heaven
> means good citizenship on earth.

> Your presence influences your city's laws,
> environment, government, and economy.

> You make it a better place to live,
> a stronger place to work,
> and a safer place to play.

You help to raise its standards,
guard its gates,
strengthen its borders,
and broaden its influence.

ROY LESSIN

*I will make them
and the places round
about my hill a blessing;
and I will cause the shower
to come down
in his season; there shall be
showers of blessing.*

EZEKIEL 34:26

God loves to surprise you with good things.

~

Like a cooling rainstorm
that suddenly appears on a hot summer's day,
God's special blessings will come upon you
in an unexpected moment.

~

He will turn an ordinary day
or a routine event
into a time of refreshing,
a wellspring of joy,
a celebration of praise.

~

He will overwhelm you with His love,
assure you with His presence,
and affirm you with His favor.
He will not do it with a few drops
or a tiny trickle,
but with a full-fledged downpour.

ROY LESSIN

*Do not repay evil
with evil or insult
with insult,
but with blessing,
because to this
you were called
so that you may
inherit a blessing.*

1 PETER 3:9 NIV

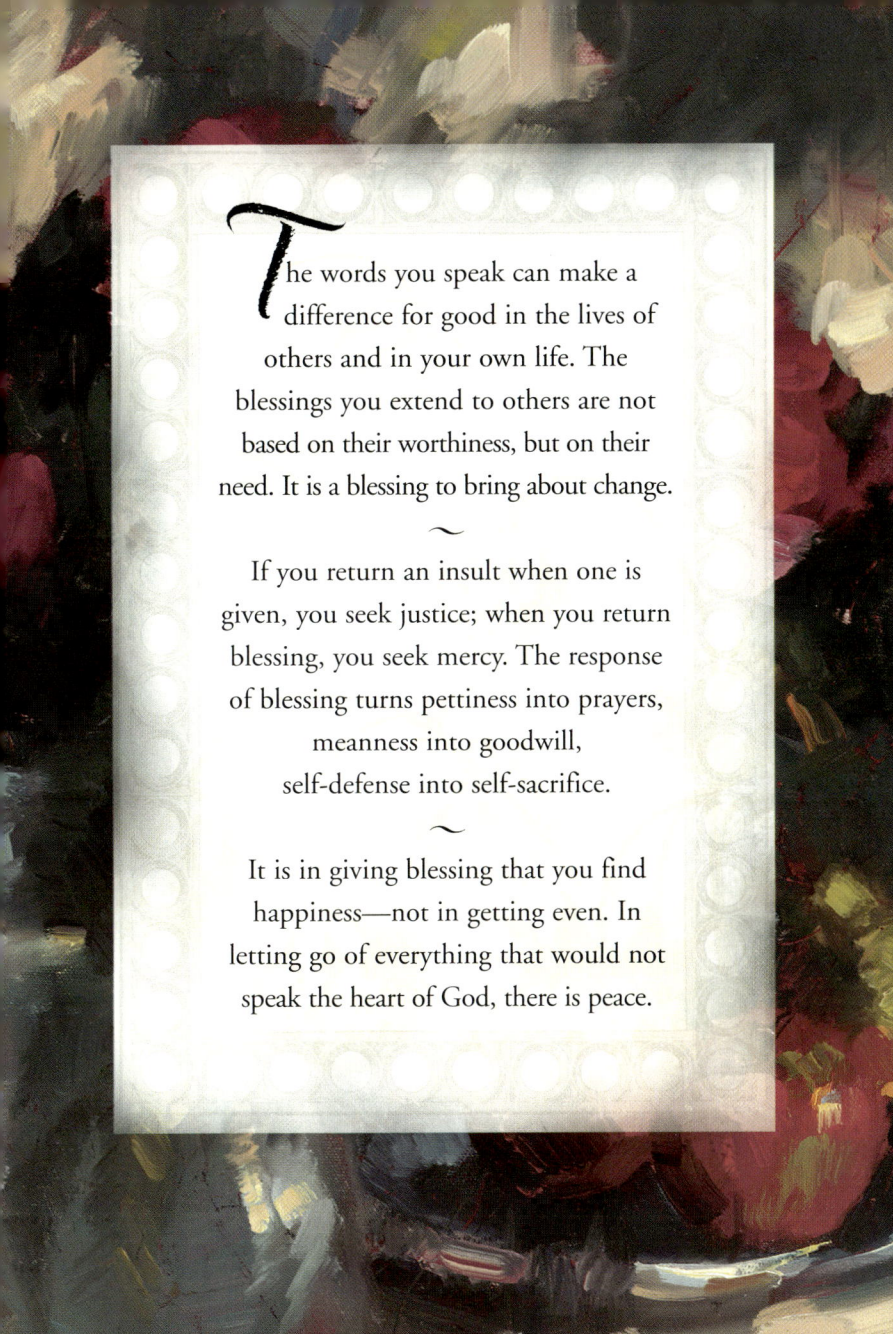

The words you speak can make a difference for good in the lives of others and in your own life. The blessings you extend to others are not based on their worthiness, but on their need. It is a blessing to bring about change.

~

If you return an insult when one is given, you seek justice; when you return blessing, you seek mercy. The response of blessing turns pettiness into prayers, meanness into goodwill, self-defense into self-sacrifice.

~

It is in giving blessing that you find happiness—not in getting even. In letting go of everything that would not speak the heart of God, there is peace.

ROY LESSIN

*I will pour water upon him
that is thirsty, and floods
upon the dry ground: I will
pour my spirit upon thy seed,
and my blessing
upon thine offspring.*

ISAIAH 44:3

Water is a blessing. When the earth drinks, things grow. When you are thirsty, the best thing to do is not to discuss water or examine its benefits; the best thing to do is drink.

~

Jesus said that He would pour out the Holy Spirit upon those who would come to Him and drink.

~

To drink is to receive, and as you do, His Spirit becomes a well of living water within you. This water not only quenches your thirst but also flows out as a river of life to bless the lives of those around you.

ROY LESSIN

*The ark of the Lord remained
in the house of Obed-Edom the Gittite
for three months, and the Lord
blessed him and his entire household.*

2 SAMUEL 6:11 NIV

The greatest blessing you bring to your family
is the presence of God in your life.

~

The fragrance of His presence
sweetens the atmosphere of your home.

~

The beauty of His presence
warms the relationships within its walls.

~

The joy of His presence
lightens every heart.

~

The glory of His presence
fills all its chambers
with rare and precious treasures.

ROY LESSIN

*From the fullness of his grace
we have all received
one blessing after another.*

JOHN 1:16 NIV

God's blessings to you in Christ are not payment for services rendered. There are not a certain number allotted to you.

~

Blessings flow from grace. Grace doesn't keep track of how much is given. It doesn't say, "I gave, so you owe me." It doesn't run out just when you need it most. Grace says, "You've just received a rich blessing—get ready for another one!"

*The memory
of the righteous
will be a blessing.*

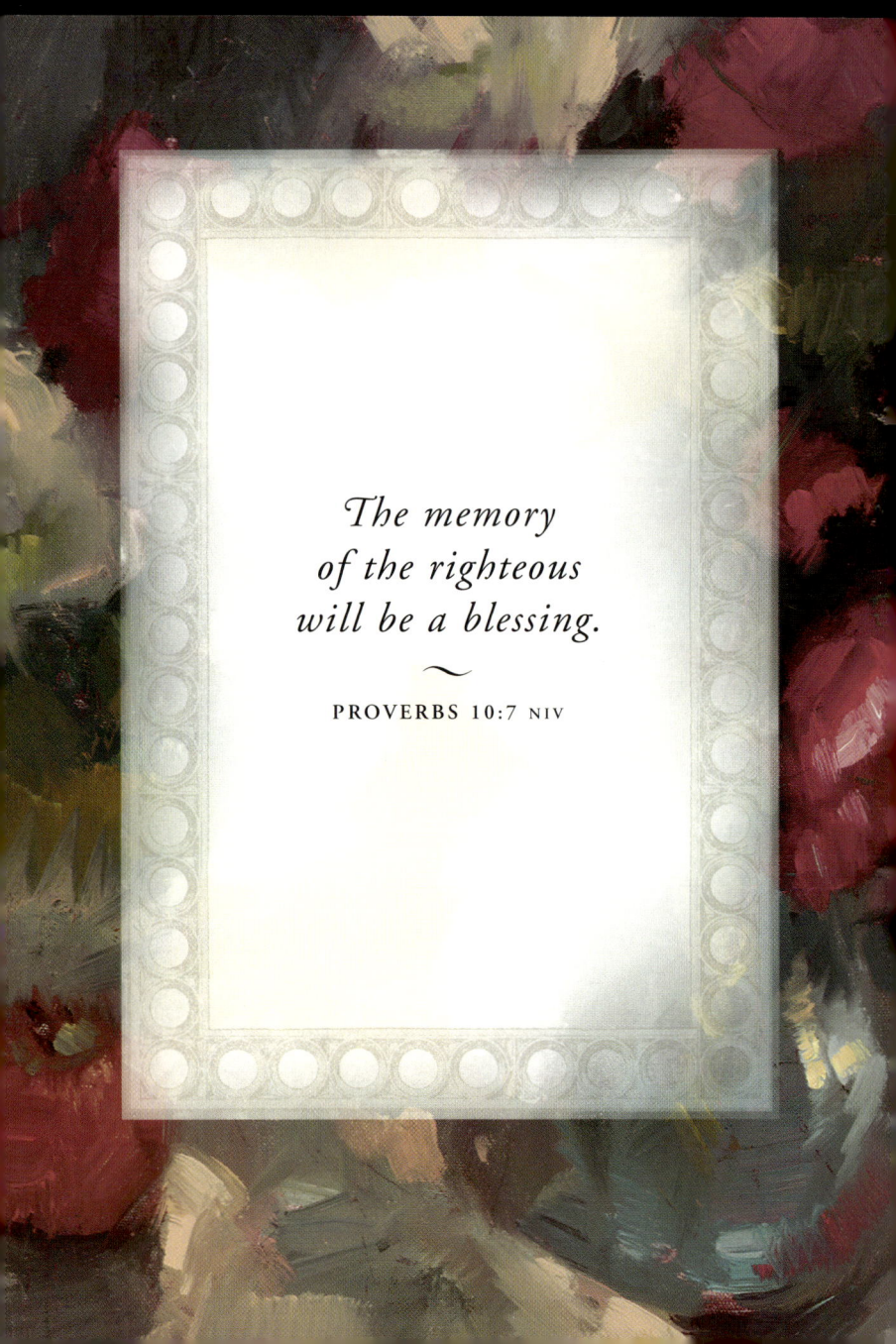

PROVERBS 10:7 NIV

God wants you to be the kind of person others enjoy thinking about. Through the example of your life and the testimony of your faith, thoughts of you will bring a smile to the hearts of others.

~

He will bless your life in such a way that a sweet remembrance of you will remain with others even after you are gone.

~

How great is the prayer, how rich is the meaning.
How full is the gratefulness of those who say,
"I thank God for you!"

*Blessed be the God and Father
of our Lord Jesus Christ,
who hath blessed us
with all spiritual blessings
in heavenly places in Christ.*

EPHESIANS 1:3

*You can receive every blessing
Heaven can offer.*

~

The spiritual riches that are yours in Christ
are beyond any value this world can place
upon them. True poverty is not determined
by the lack of someone's bank account, but
by the bankruptcy in spirit that results from a
life void of the presence of Christ.

~

He has placed within you riches that can never
decay or be stolen, riches that are the
foundations of joy, riches that will abide with
you always, and riches that will forever endure.

ROY LESSIN

*They were pleased to do it,
and indeed they owe it to them.
For if the Gentiles have shared
in the Jews' spiritual blessings,
they owe it to the Jews
to share with them their
material blessings.*

ROMANS 15:27 NIV

You can impart two types of blessings to others. One is spiritual; the other is material. Both are important.

∼

God wants all of His people to be so heavenly minded that they truly are of earthly good. Through spiritual blessings, you extend God's heart to others; through material blessings you extend His hand.

∼

Spiritual blessings reveal His heart; material blessings reveal His compassion. Spiritual blessings meet the needs of time and eternity; material blessings meet the needs of today.

Bring ye all the tithes into the storehouse, that there may be meat in mine house, and prove me now herewith, saith the Lord of hosts, if I will not open you the windows of heaven, and pour you out a blessing, that there shall not be room enough to receive it.

MALACHI 3:10

*Pour a gallon of water over a bucket,
and most of the water lands in the bucket.*

*Pour the same gallon of water over a pop bottle,
and only a small portion will make its way inside.*

The difference in the two vessels is their capacity to receive.

*God's calls of obedience in your life do not increase
His capacity to bless you;
they are given to increase your capacity to receive.*

*An open hand can hold more than a closed one.
A soft heart can absorb more than a hard one.
A thirsty soul will drink more than a self-satisfied one.*

*I am sure that,
when I come unto you,
I shall come in the fulness
of the blessing
of the gospel of Christ.*

ROMANS 15:29

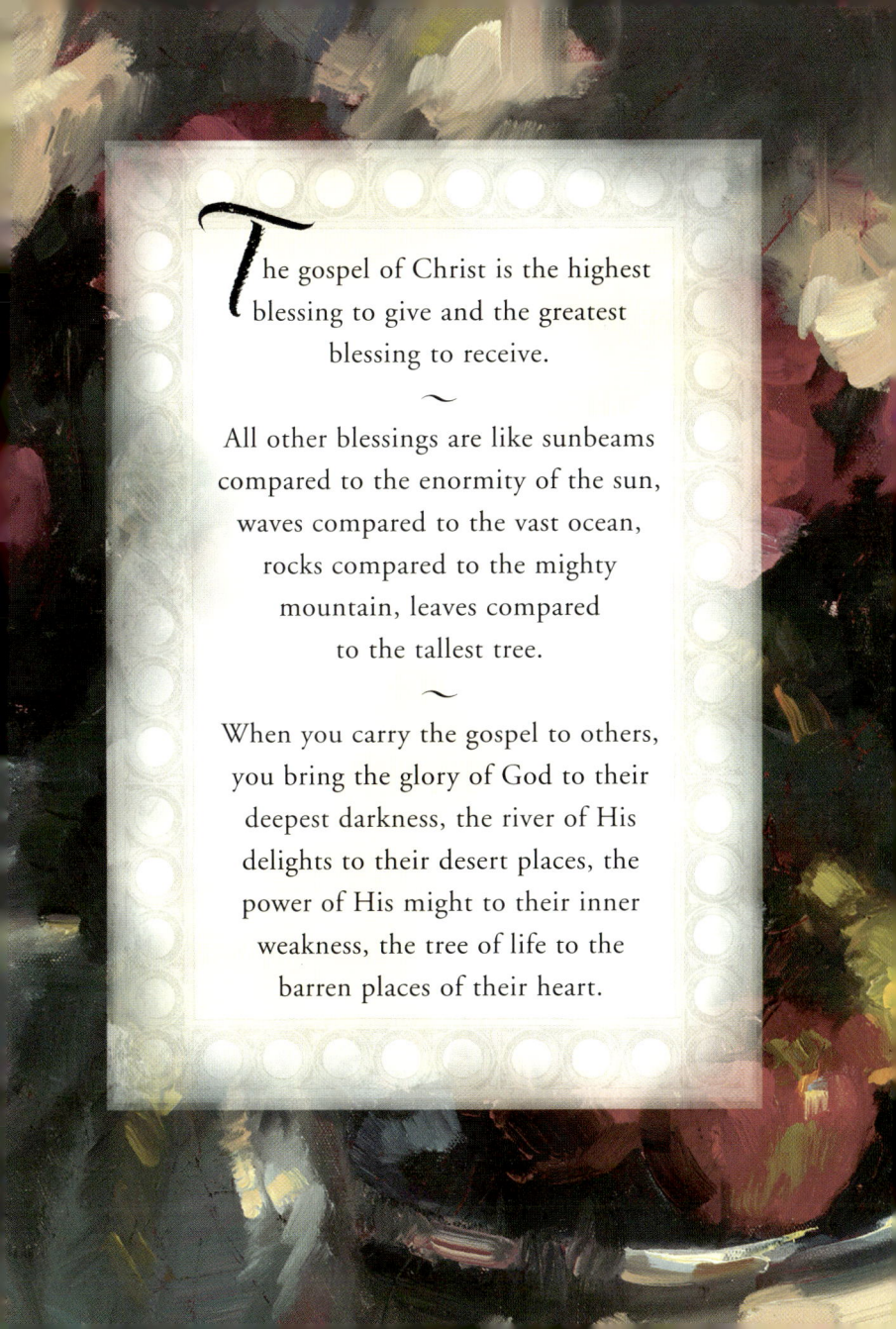

The gospel of Christ is the highest blessing to give and the greatest blessing to receive.

~

All other blessings are like sunbeams compared to the enormity of the sun, waves compared to the vast ocean, rocks compared to the mighty mountain, leaves compared to the tallest tree.

~

When you carry the gospel to others, you bring the glory of God to their deepest darkness, the river of His delights to their desert places, the power of His might to their inner weakness, the tree of life to the barren places of their heart.

ROY LESSIN

*Jacob replied,
"I will not let you go
unless you bless me."*

GENESIS 32:26 NIV

Holding on to God for blessing is not a struggle to change God's mind; it is a demonstration of how much you value the reign of His kingdom upon your life.

~

Jesus said His "kingdom . . . has been forcefully advancing, and forceful men lay hold of it" (Matthew 11:12 NIV). As you wrap your arms of faith around Him, you are saying, "Where else can I go, Lord, for only You have the words of eternal life." (See John 6:68.)

ROY LESSIN

If a fellow Hebrew, a man or a woman, sells himself to you and serves you six years, in the seventh year you must let him go free. And when you release him, do not send him away empty-handed. Supply him liberally from your flock, your threshing floor and your winepress. Give to him as the Lord your God has blessed you.

DEUTERONOMY 15:12-14 NIV

When God asks you to extend blessing, it is often for two important reasons. One is to touch someone's life with love; the other is to be a reminder of how much God has touched your life with His love.

It is good for each of us to remember where we have come from and how far God has taken us. By His grace, you have what you have, you are where you are, and you will become all He desires you to be. God wants your giving to be done in the same way and with the same attitude that He gives.

Give happily and freely.
Give what is needed.
Give abundantly.

ROY LESSIN

*Bless all his skills,
O LORD, and be pleased
with the work of his hands.*

DEUTERONOMY 33:11 NIV

It is wonderful to know that God not only gives you the gifts and skills you possess, but He also will bless them, sharpen them, and make them highly effective.

~

His blessing can extend to your work and business relationships. He will open doors and give you favor. He will give you solutions to perplexing problems. He will change hearts and bring the right people into your life.

~

His timing will be perfect and His ways past finding out.

ROY LESSIN

*At that time the Lord
set apart the tribe of Levi
to carry the ark of the covenant
of the Lord, to stand
before the Lord to minister
and to pronounce blessings
in his name, as they still do today.*

DEUTERONOMY 10:8 NIV

There are people whose lives
will be touched as you pronounce
blessing upon them.

What a privilege it is to extend the
blessing of God to others!

Proclaim it through your words,
extend it through your hands,
declare it through your prayers.

Bless the kind, the needy, the unlovely.
Bless the friend, the family member, the stranger.
Bless the strong, the weak, the weary.
Bless the seeker, the doubter,
and all the household of God.

*About Joseph he said:
"May the Lord bless his land
with the precious dew
from heaven above and with
the deep waters that lie below."*

DEUTERONOMY 33:13 NIV

One of the great blessings of God that comes to you is inner rest. As the dew only settles when the night winds are still, so His refreshment comes as our spirits are quiet before Him—free of strife, worry, anxiety, and fear.

∼

Rest is the blessing of calm in the midst of life's storms,
trust in times of uncertainty,
assurance in times of doubt.

∼

Deep within you will run quiet waters
beside peaceful shores.

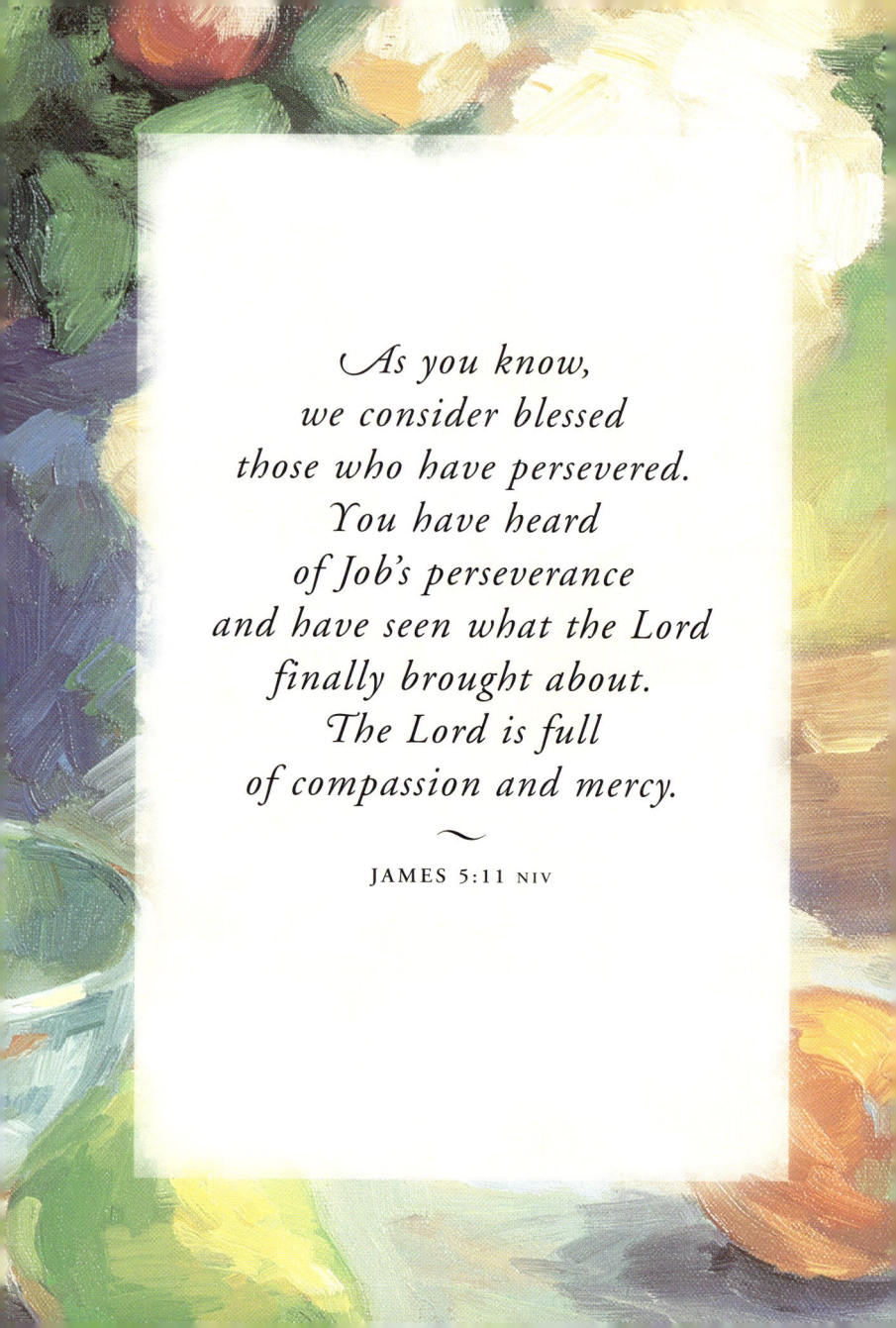

*As you know,
we consider blessed
those who have persevered.
You have heard
of Job's perseverance
and have seen what the Lord
finally brought about.
The Lord is full
of compassion and mercy.*

~

JAMES 5:11 NIV

You bless others as your life bears testimony to the faithfulness of God. God will take you through difficult times not only to test your faith and strengthen your character, but also to be a source of comfort and encouragement to others.

~

Through your perseverance, they will see that it is better to hold on to His promises than to let go of their trust, wiser to let Him make the decisions than for them to follow their own way, greater to leave the end of all things with Him than to take matters into their own hands.

*Then Peter said, Lo,
we have left all,
and followed thee.
And he said unto them,
Verily I say unto you,
There is no man
that hath left house,
or parents, or brethren,
or wife, or children,
for the kingdom
of God's sake,
Who shall not receive manifold
more in this present time,
and in the world to come
life everlasting.*

LUKE 18:28-30

The richest blessings of God in your life are best
understood, not by what it cost you to follow Him,
but by understanding all you have gained
in obeying His call.

～

To go where He leads you means you have taken the
higher ground. To take up your cross means you
have drawn closer to His heart. To keep your hand
to the plow means your eye is set on greater riches.

～

Like Abraham, you look for a city to come;
like Peter, you are a pilgrim whose journey
leads to an inheritance that can never perish;
like Paul, you count all things but loss to gain Christ
—the pearl of greatest price!

ROY LESSIN

*The man
who looks intently
into the perfect law
that gives freedom,
and continues to do this,
not forgetting
what he has heard,
but doing it
—he will be blessed
in what he does.*

JAMES 1:25 NIV

*D*oing is blessing.

The Word moves you into faith,
and faith moves you into action.
The action will be for good,
and the glory will be for God.

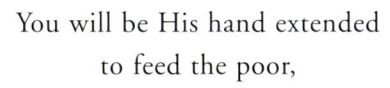

You will be His hand extended
to feed the poor,
to comfort the widow,
to shelter the orphan,
to lift the oppressed,
to deliver the captive, and
to loose those who are bound.

The blessing of the Word will lead you
to show love to your neighbor,
to visit those in prison,
and to give a cup of cold water in His name.

ROY LESSIN

*Surely you have granted him
eternal blessings and made him
glad with the joy of your presence.*

PSALM 21:6 NIV

What a blessing it is to live
with eternity's values in view.

~

To have your eye set on the goal,
to have your heart fixed on the calling,
to have your will set on the prize.
To know that the best is yet to be.
To plan with purpose.
To walk in hope.
To live with meaning.

~

The Father's voice keeps you moving,
the coming of His kingdom keeps you marching,
and the glory of His presence
keeps you longing for home.

ROY LESSIN

*In everything I did,
I showed you that
by this kind of hard work
we must help the weak,
remembering the words
the Lord Jesus himself said:
"It is more blessed
to give than to receive."*

ACTS 20:35 NIV

$\mathcal{I}$n God's economy when you give, you gain.

~

You gain blessings of joy and gladness of heart.
You gain the satisfaction of seeing a need met.
You gain treasures in heaven and the increase to give again.

~

When God puts you in a position that requires you
to receive from another, do it with graciousness, with
gratefulness, and with humility. Don't deny the
other person the blessing of giving to you.

ROY LESSIN

*Blessed are they
whose transgressions
are forgiven,
whose sins are covered.
Blessed is the man
whose sin
the Lord will never
count against him.*

ROMANS 4:7-8 NIV

FROM GOD'S HEART TO YOURS

What a blessing it is to be forgiven. It frees you from the guilt of the past and the judgment of the future. It unlocks the shackles that kept you in bondage and breaks the cords of regret that had you bound. It pulls you out of the horrible pit of despair and places your feet on the solid ground of hopefulness. It washes the stains that soiled your spirit and cleanses your heart from its wandering ways.

~

Begin each day with the joy of knowing you are forgiven.

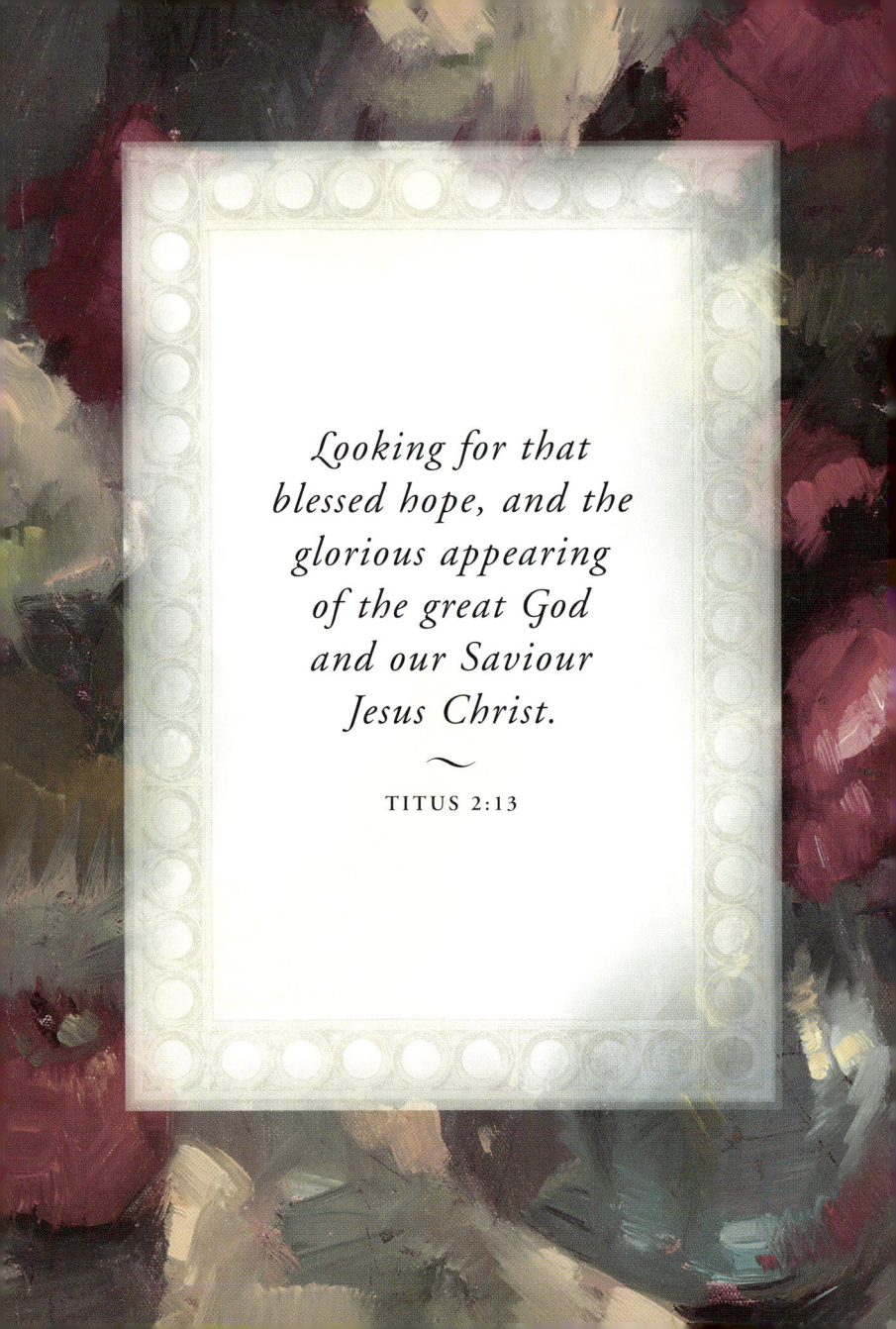

Looking for that blessed hope, and the glorious appearing of the great God and our Saviour Jesus Christ.

TITUS 2:13

FROM GOD'S HEART TO YOURS

You have been blessed with the "blessed hope."

~

Many people in the world are without hope;
others have "a hope,"
but only God's child has the flame
of the blessed hope burning inside.

~

It is a hope based on truth.
It is a hope sealed by the resurrection
of Jesus Christ from the dead.
It is a hope guaranteed by the Holy Spirit,
reserved in Heaven for you.
It is the hope of the resurrection of the body;
it is the hope of life eternal;
it is the hope of His appearing;
it is the hope of the bride waiting for the bridegroom;
it is the hope of the guest invited to the great banquet;
it is the hope of the worshiper longing
to be at his Master's feet.

ROY LESSIN

*He took the children
in his arms,
put his hands on them
and blessed them.*

MARK 10:16 NIV

Children need blessing in their lives.
In a world where so much is against them,
they need to know that God is for them;
at a time when so many children are unwanted,
they need to know the Father cares.
You can bless them with your time,
your attention, and your affection.
You can bless them with your words,
your correction, and your example.
You can bless them by being a teacher,
a counselor, and a friend.
You can bless them by bringing them to Jesus,
the One who loves them most of all.

ROY LESSIN

Blessed is she who has believed that what the Lord has said to her will be accomplished!

LUKE 1:45 NIV

Great happiness comes
to the heart that is trusting God.

~

To doubt God is to question His character; to question God is to doubt His Word. Trust keeps you from holding back. It helps you embrace His Word with a total "yes" and release all things into His hands.

~

The blessings of rest are peace to your soul, rest to your spirit, and joy to your heart. You will be blessed as you listen to Him. You will be blessed as you wait on Him. Most of all, you will be blessed with the answer that comes from Him.

*Blessed are the merciful:
for they shall obtain mercy.*

MATTHEW 5:7

One of the great blessings of mercy
is that it triumphs over judgment.
Mercy delivers from the sin of revenge
or the burden of "getting even."
Mercy is extended, never deserved.
Mercy is pity instead of penalty,
compassion instead of condemnation,
release instead of retaliation.

~

Mercy does not demand payment for the consequence of sin.
Mercy is the pathway to pardon and the gateway to grace.
Mercy is extending to others everything God has extended to you.

ROY LESSIN

*Blessed is the man
whom God corrects;
so do not despise
the discipline
of the Almighty.*

JOB 5:17 NIV

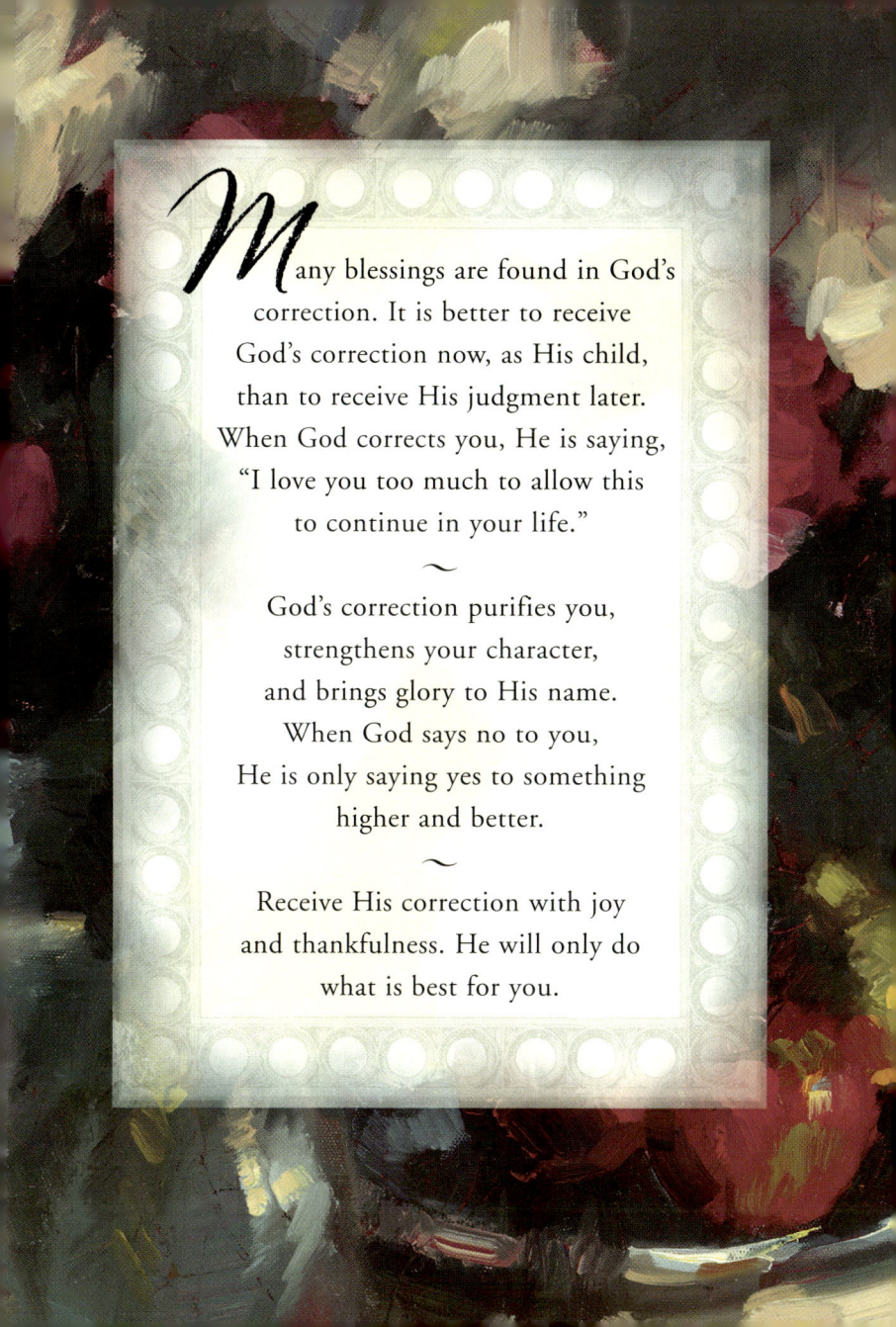

Many blessings are found in God's
correction. It is better to receive
God's correction now, as His child,
than to receive His judgment later.
When God corrects you, He is saying,
"I love you too much to allow this
to continue in your life."

∼

God's correction purifies you,
strengthens your character,
and brings glory to His name.
When God says no to you,
He is only saying yes to something
higher and better.

∼

Receive His correction with joy
and thankfulness. He will only do
what is best for you.

ROY LESSIN

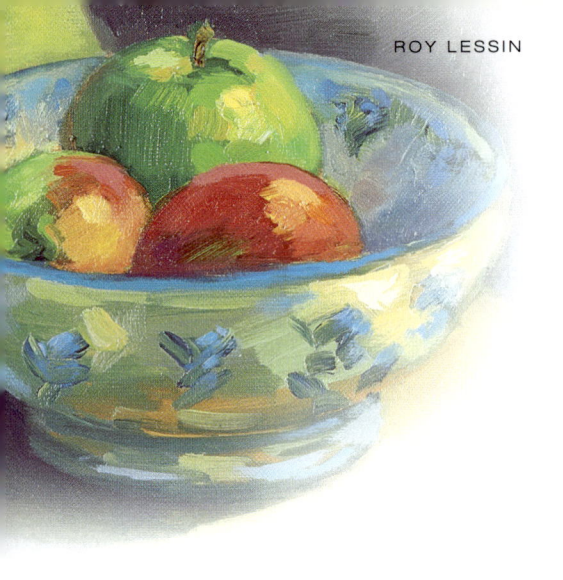

*Your basket and your
kneading trough
will be blessed.*

DEUTERONOMY 28:5 NIV

The blessing of the Lord extends to the place where food is gathered and prepared. The kitchen truly is the home's special place—a place where people love to gather, where bread is broken, and where hearts can freely share. It is the place of ministry, where caring hands serve and giving hearts reach out to others' needs. Its atmosphere fills the home with warmth, with rich aromas, and with thanksgiving.

It is the place of communion, fellowship, and hospitality.
It is the happy place, the welcome place,
the bountiful place, the creative place.

How rich is the home
that is filled with its blessings.

*Blessed is the man
that walketh not
in the counsel
of the ungodly,
nor standeth
in the way of sinners,
nor sitteth in the seat
of the scornful.*

PSALM 1:1

God's wisdom is not only different than the world's, but it is past finding out. God gives His wisdom to those who fear Him and to those who ask in faith.

The wise see life through God's eyes, think His thoughts, and know His ways. The blessing of God's wisdom keeps you from foolish ways and wrong choices.

The wisdom of God seeks peaceful paths and causes you to live with eternity's values in view. His wisdom is more precious than gold and sweeter than honey from the comb. It is sure and trustworthy, pure and radiant, perfect and right.

Following His wisdom brings great reward.

ROY LESSIN

*He who despises
his neighbor sins,
but blessed is he
who is kind
to the needy.*

PROVERBS 14:21 NIV

Kindness is one of the great blessings of life.

~

It builds bridges instead of walls.
It finds ways to heal instead of hurt.
It seeks ways to build up instead of tear down.
It looks for ways to encourage instead of disappoint.

~

The eyes of kindness see others' needs;
the heart of kindness reaches out to touch,
to help, and to support.

~

Kindness mellows hardness, bends stiffness,
warms coldness, and smooths roughness.
Kindness changes the disposition of the serpent
into the nature of the dove
and the judge into a minister of mercy.

ROY LESSIN

*Blessed is the man
who listens to me,
watching daily at my doors,
waiting at my doorway.*

PROVERBS 8:34 NIV

Special blessings are yours
when God has your attention
and you give God time.
He wants you to move
on His schedule and at His pace.
He wants you to be at rest and at peace.
He wants your waiting times
to be growing times.
He wants you to be still
and know that He is in control.
He is never late.

~

Wait quietly.
Wait patiently.
Wait attentively.

~

He makes all things beautiful in His time.

*A faithful man
shall abound
with blessings.*

PROVERBS 28:20

FROM GOD'S HEART TO YOURS

*H*ow blessed are the lives of those who have a faithful friend,
faithful parents, a faithful wife or husband, a faithful coworker,
or a faithful brother or sister in Christ.

~

The faithful can be depended upon and their word can be trusted.
The blessing of faithfulness is "being there" at the time of need,
"standing there" at the time of uncertainty,
"remaining there" at the time of adversity.

~

It is being constant when things are changing,
firm when things are lax,
true when things are dishonest,
steady when things are shaking.

~

Through faithfulness, words are never idle,
trust is never lost, loyalty is never forsaken.

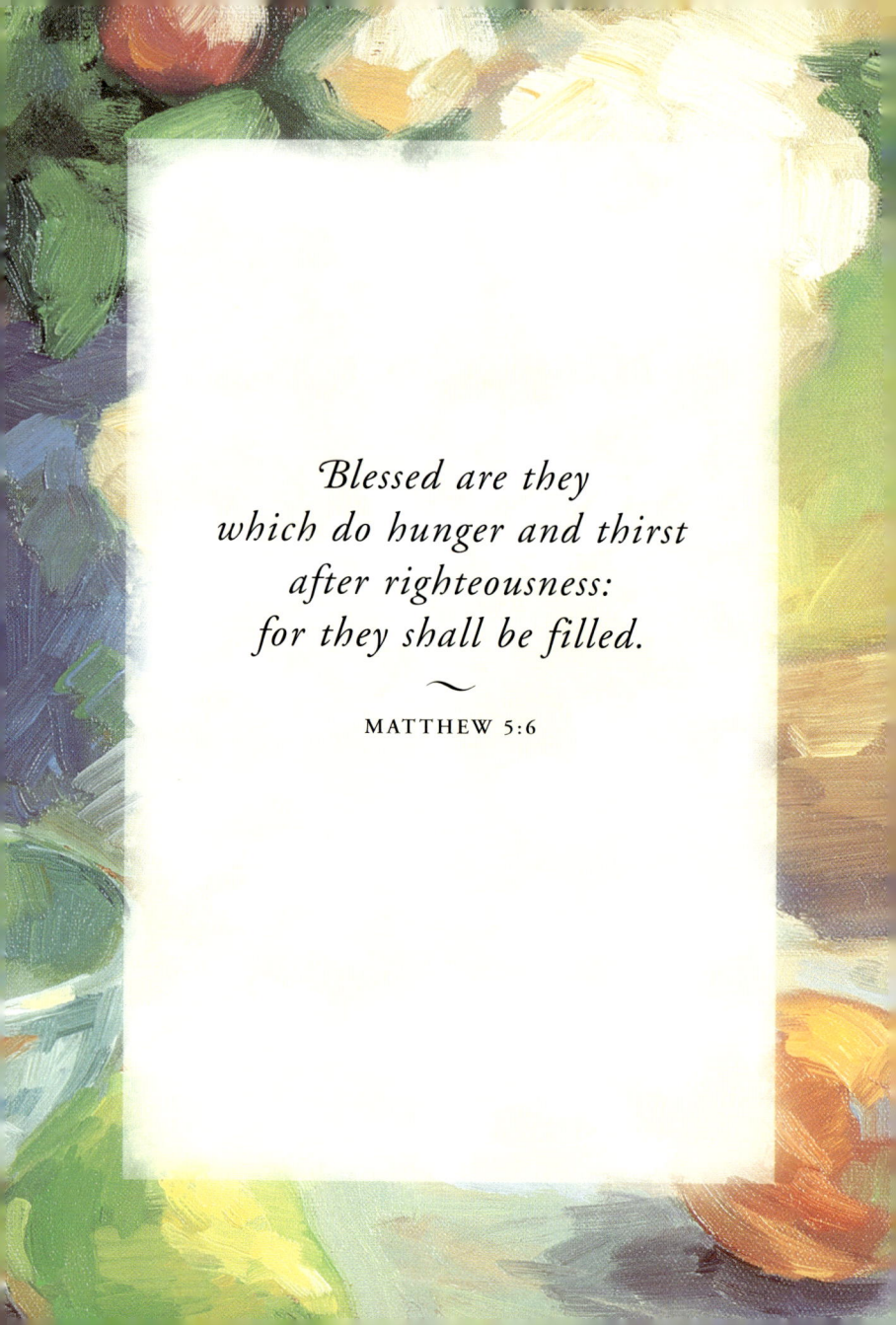

*Blessed are they
which do hunger and thirst
after righteousness:
for they shall be filled.*

MATTHEW 5:6

The blessed life that God has for you is a full one
—rich in mercy, generous in grace,
mighty in power, clean in holiness,
strong in purpose, bountiful in blessing.

As you hunger for it, you will be filled with the bread of Heaven;
as you thirst for it, you will drink of the water of life.
It is the life abundant, overflowing with His goodness;
the life triumphant, infused with His strength;
the life magnificent, beautified with His presence.
It is the blessed life that quickens your spirit,
that touches your soul, that lifts your countenance,
that gladdens your heart.

It is the life of wholeness,
the life of fruitfulness,
the life of love.

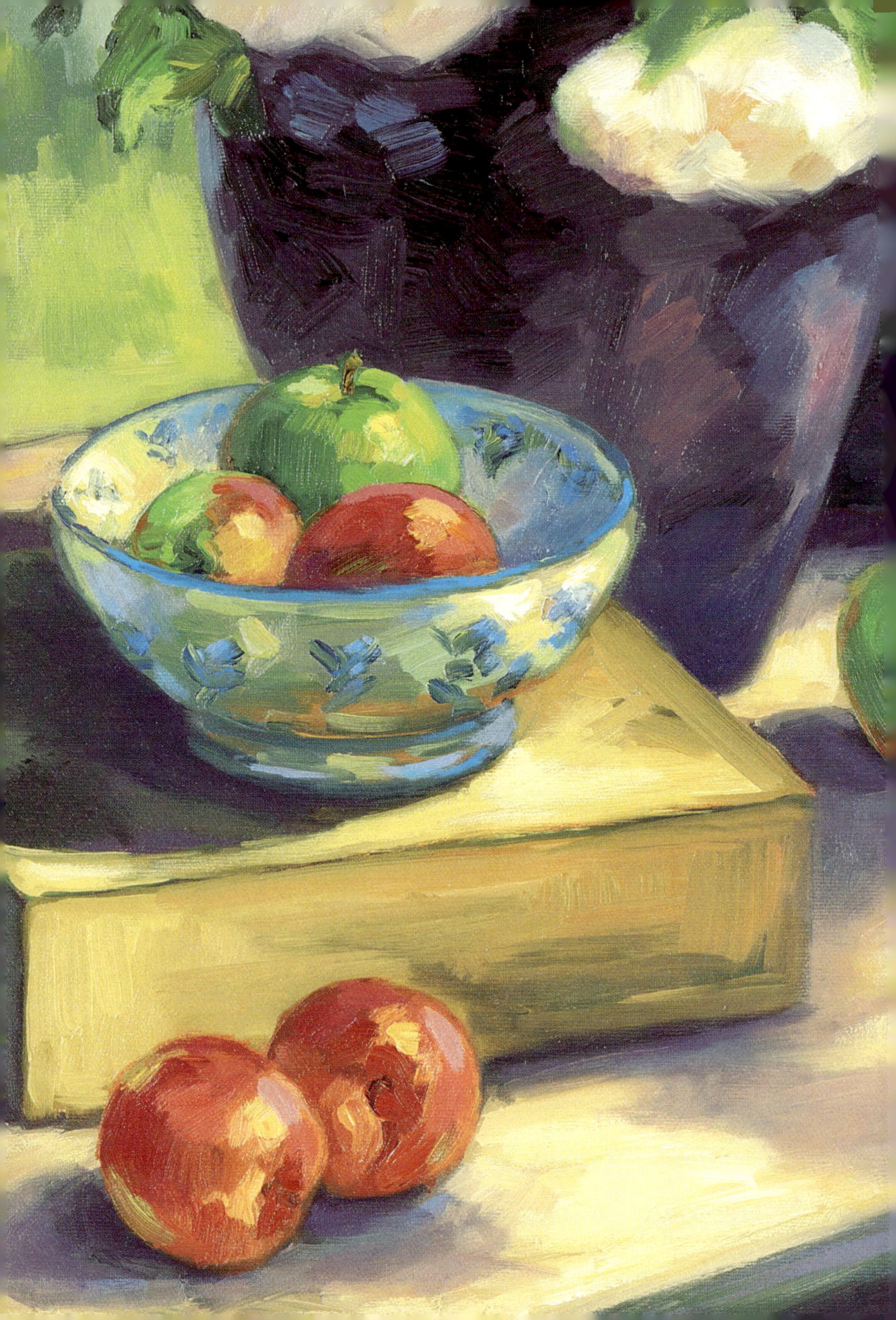

ROY LESSIN IS A CO-FOUNDER OF DAYSPRING CARDS, THE PREMIER US CHRISTIAN CARD COMPANY. HE IS THE AUTHOR OF MORE THAN A DOZEN BOOKS, INCLUDING *FORGIVEN*, WHICH WAS A FINALIST FOR A GOLD MEDALLION AWARD FOR BEST INSPIRATIONAL BOOK. LESSIN IS A GRADUATE OF BETHANY COLLEGE OF MISSIONS AND HAS BEEN ACTIVE IN MISSION WORK, CHRISTIAN EDUCATION, AND COUNSELLING. HE IS A SENIOR WRITER FOR DAYSPRING AND LIVES WITH HIS WIFE IN SILOAM SPRINGS, ARKANSAS.

Additional copies of this book
are available from your local bookstore.

Also by Roy Lessin:
Always Loved, Never Forgotten

If you have enjoyed this book, or if it has
impacted your life, we would like to hear from you.

Please contact us at:
Eagle Publishing Limited
6 Kestrel House,
Mill Street,
Trowbridge,
BA14 8BE